EUROPA  MILITARI

101st AIRBORNE DIVISION
IN COLOUR PHOTOGRAPHS

BARRY D.SMITH

Windrow & Greene

AIR ASSAULT DIVISION

One look at Campbell Army Airfield at Ft.Campbell, Kentucky, reveals that the division stationed here is no ordinary formation. Dominated by a runway long enough to accomodate the largest transport aircraft in the USAF fleet, it is also home to the 350 helicopters operated by the 101st Airborne Division (Air Assault) - the only division of its kind in the world.

The 101st is the ultimate refinement of the airborne concept. When the philosophy of "vertical envelopment" was first tested in combat in World War II the helicopter was in its infancy, and not yet a practical item of mass-production military hardware; troops and equipment were parachuted from transport aircraft or landed in gliders. With the wide availability of reliable, versatile helicopters in the early 1960s the US Army finally had a true airborne vehicle, at a time when the practical and cost/effect disadvantages of the old

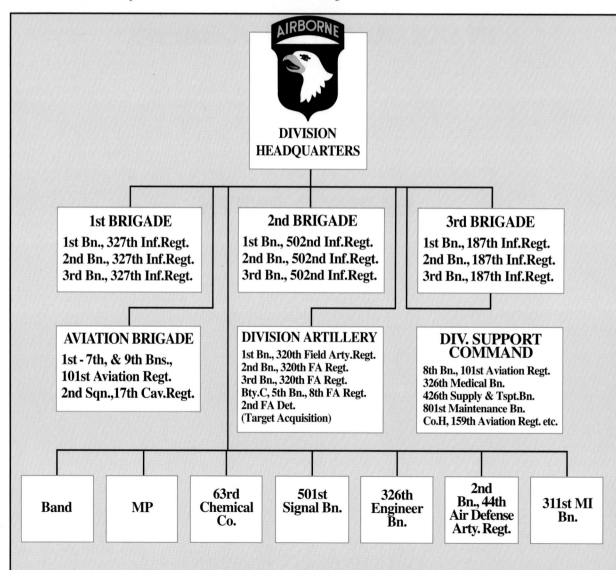

DIVISION HEADQUARTERS

1st BRIGADE
1st Bn., 327th Inf.Regt.
2nd Bn., 327th Inf.Regt.
3rd Bn., 327th Inf.Regt.

2nd BRIGADE
1st Bn., 502nd Inf.Regt.
2nd Bn., 502nd Inf.Regt.
3rd Bn., 502nd Inf.Regt.

3rd BRIGADE
1st Bn., 187th Inf.Regt.
2nd Bn., 187th Inf.Regt.
3rd Bn., 187th Inf.Regt.

AVIATION BRIGADE
1st - 7th, & 9th Bns.,
101st Aviation Regt.
2nd Sqn.,17th Cav.Regt.

DIVISION ARTILLERY
1st Bn., 320th Field Arty.Regt.
2nd Bn., 320th FA Regt.
3rd Bn., 320th FA Regt.
Bty.C, 5th Bn., 8th FA Regt.
2nd FA Det.
(Target Acquisition)

DIV. SUPPORT COMMAND
8th Bn., 101st Aviation Regt.
326th Medical Bn.
426th Supply & Tspt.Bn.
801st Maintenance Bn.
Co.H, 159th Aviation Regt. etc.

Band

MP

63rd Chemical Co.

501st Signal Bn.

326th Engineer Bn.

2nd Bn., 44th Air Defense Arty. Regt.

311st MI Bn.

(Opposite) The 101st Division shoulder patch shows an American bald eagle on a black shield, under the 1942 "Airborne" tab. The emblem was first adopted in 1923 by the 101st Infantry Division when it was based in the state of Wisconsin. The eagle head represented "Old Abe", the eagle mascot of the 8th Wisconsin Infantry Regiment which was carried into battle with the regimental colors during the American Civil War. Indeed, from 1942 to 1956 the Division kept a live bald eagle as a mascot.

(Right) Monument at the foot of the flag pole at the Headquarters building of the 101st Airborne at Fort Campbell, Kentucky. The UH-l "Huey" helicopter is the symbol of the Division's mobility. Today the Huey has almost disappeared from the Division's inventory, replaced by the more powerful and capable UH-60A Black Hawk.

World War II-style multi-unit parachute assault were being addressed in many armies.

The infantry of the 101st are organized into three brigades each of three battalions. These units are supported by an artillery brigade comprising three battalions equipped with towed 105mm howitzers. A separate air defense artillery battalion fields Stinger missiles and Vulcan 20mm "Gatling" guns. There are no tanks, self-propelled artillery or armored personnel carriers assigned to the 101st: all weapon systems in the Division must be capable of being airlifted by helicopter, either internally or as external slung loads, accompanied by their crews and ammunition.

The Division's aviation brigade contains the helicopter units. While a normal division might have two or three helicopter battalions, the 101st has no less than eight, plus an air cavalry squadron. What makes the 101st unique is not only the number of helicopters, however, but how they use them.

The helicopters are tied into a concept that the US Army calls "combined arms". They are a tool, just like the artillery and the infantry, to accomplish a mission: the helicopters are assigned to the ground commanders to use as they see fit until the mission is completed. The ground commander's staff includes aviation officers who can advise him on how best to use the helicopter assets under any particular circumstances. This gives the ground commander the greatest possible flexibility to exploit gains, or to redeploy if a unit gets into trouble. In other divisions the units request aviation support from their aviation brigade, and may never see the aviation staff; and after the helicopters perform a task they report back to their own headquarters for another assignment.

Another unique feature of the Division

(Above) UH-60A helicopter of the 101st Aviation Brigade being loaded into a giant USAF C-5 Galaxy transport; in the foreground, a C-130 Hercules transport. This is a common sight at Campbell Army Airfield; the USAF works closely with the Division in many areas - providing the transports to deploy the 101st overseas, delivering supplies in the combat zone, attacking objectives in concert with the Division, and providing air cover for its deployed units. The massive Galaxy can even accomodate two CH-47D Chinook helicopters, with their rotors removed and parts of the upper fuselage disassembled.

(Inset) The Air Assault badge, featuring a winged UH-l helicopter, worn by graduates of the Air Assault School. Every member of the Division is supposed to go through the School, from the commanding general, to the helicopter pilots, to the newest infantry private. Soldiers who have graduated from both paratrooper jump school and the Air Assault course say that this badge is tougher to win than "jump wings".

5

Physical fitness is naturally emphasized throughout any formation with an Airborne heritage, and constant exercise keeps all ranks sharp. Here troopers pound past the HQ building, carrying unit flags.
(Photo courtesy 101st AA Division)

be working together on a given mission.

Obviously, no air-deployed and therefore relatively lightly equipped division is expected to withstand a frontal assault by an enemy armored division. The 101st uses its mobility to strike and move before the enemy can react with an organized attack. The lack of armor does not leave the Division helpless against enemy tanks and APCs, however: TOW anti-tank units mounted on Humm Vees, and TOW and Hellfire launchers fitted to AH-1E Cobra and AH-64 Apache helicopters, provide a powerful integral anti-armor force.

As part of the US Central Command (the former "Rapid Deployment Force") under XVIII Airborne Corps, the Division has contingency plans for operating anywhere in the world at short notice. One "ready battalion" is constantly on the alert, and can be ready to move within 18 hours. It would take ten to 14 days for the entire 101st to deploy; this is slower than the 82nd Airborne Division, because transporting the large number of helicopters over long distances inevitably takes time. Once in-theater, however, the Division can move with amazing speed and power.

The 101st needs a high level of logistical support during combat; the whole formation can consume as much as 450,000 gallons of jet fuel every day of battle. Since the "teeth" units travel as light as possible, a significant percentage of the helicopters are used for resupply once combat operations begin. This effort is augmented by support from USAF C-130 Hercules and C-141 Starlifter transports, either dropping supplies by parachute or landing on rough airfields carved out by the Division.

The advantages of such a powerful mobile force far outweigh the logistical drawbacks. Terrain features mean nothing to the 101st; they simply bypass natural obstacles, or use them to their advantage. Heavily fortified areas can just as easily be avoided. No enemy can be strong everywhere simultaneously; the 101st finds a vulnerable spot, and appears there with sudden violence. Since it is so mobile the Division needs little or no reserve forces, and can use all available units in an attack. Units can then be shifted round the battlefield by helicopter, to exploit openings or to reinforce other elements. By constantly striking and then moving the 101st can prevent the enemy from forming any accurate idea of the attacking force's strength, location, or true objectives.

is "habitual association". The same aviation units are assigned to the same infantry brigades on every mission, whether for training or for actual combat. This allows a close working relationship to grow up between the staffs and the field units. This is true not only for the aviation assets, but for all the different units: artillery, air defense, etc. This "macro-buddy system" makes each infantry brigade and its supporting arms a familiar team of players rather than just a group of units that happen to

Another way in which the 101st counters the enemy's defenses is to fight by night as often as possible. All the helicopter crews use night vision goggles to "see" in the dark. By day the greatest threat to low-flying helicopters is not necessarily the sophisticated surface-to-air missile system, but the ordinary footsoldier firing a rifle or machine gun. Under cover of darkness, and hugging the ground, helicopters are very difficult to spot. Using the terrain to avoid radar detection and darkness to shield them from ground fire, they can accomplish their missions with a much higher degree of safety. The attack helicopters, too, have special night vision and electronic systems which allow them to acquire and destroy targets while remaining unseen themselves.

The concept of the air assault division has gained attention throughout the world, and although few other armies have the material resources to follow suit, many countries have sent representatives to study the 101st's methods. In Europe a multinational air assault formation is being planned as a NATO quick reaction force. While expensive to operate, the 101st Airborne (Air Assault) is a highly mobile and powerful asset that can strike deep into enemy territory. Considering the instability that plagues the world in the aftermath of the collapse of so many long-established Communist and Communist-satellite governments, it is fortunate indeed that the United States boasts such a formation in its armory.

(Above) Memorial to the veterans of the 187th Infantry Regiment, which today makes up the Division's 3rd Brigade; it is the only US airborne regiment which fought in World War 2, Korea, and Vietnam. The nickname "Rakkasans", Japanese for "falling umbrellas from the sky", was acquired while the regiment was on occupation duty in Japan following World War 2.

(Right) Statue on the front steps of the 101st's Headquarters building at Ft.Campbell, symbolizing the Division's global reach. The Division has been a spearhead formation of the US Army's strategic rapid deployment force since the late 1950s, under that organization's successive titles (Strategic Army Corps, Army Strike Command, Rapid Deployment Force, and currently US Central Command).

THE HISTORY OF THE 101st

The 101st Airborne Division (Air Assault) can trace its lineage to the 101st Division formed in July 1918 to fight in France in World War I. When the war ended shortly thereafter the Division was disbanded in December 1918. The 101st Infantry Division was organized in 1921 as a reserve formation headquartered in Milwaukee, Wisconsin.

In July 1942, nearly two years after the activation of the US Army's first airborne combat unit (the 501st Parachute Infantry Battalion), Army Ground Forces recommended the formation of two airborne divisions: the 82nd and 101st, to be formed by splitting the 82nd Infantry Division, then in training as a motorized division at Camp Claiborne, La. The new formations were to be smaller than infantry divisions (about 8,400 men, as against more than 15,000), initially comprising one three-battalion parachute infantry regiment; two two-battalion glider infantry regiments; two parachute and two glider field artillery battalions each with 12 howitzers; small support elements, and just 650 light vehicles. Training began at Ft.Bragg that September.

Reconstruction: paratrooper of the 101st Airborne Division preparing to emplane on a C-47 for the D-Day landings, June 1944. His M1942 paratrooper's field coat bears a national flag right shoulder patch, as worn in World War 2 for quick identification in multi-national operations in enemy occupied territory. Taped to the camouflage net of his M1C parachutist's helmet, with A-straps and leather chincup, is the paratrooper first aid packet containing a field dressing, tourniquet and morphine syrette. For operations in coastal areas he wears a B4 life vest under the harness of his T5 parachute. A Thompson M1 sub-machine gun with 20-round magazine is thrust reversed under the broad waist webbing of the harness; a general purpose ammunition bag (designed to take 19 different types of ammo) is slung on his right hip, over a rope skein, a holstered M1911A1 semi-auto pistol and a fighting knife. His M1936 musette bag, serving as a field pack, is slung beneath his reserve chute for the jump. (Photo courtesy Tim Hawkins, from the forthcoming "The World War 2 GI: US Army Uniforms 1941-45", ISBN 1872004644, pub.Windrow & Greene Ltd., Nov.1993)

While the mix of units could be varied, and extra units were later assigned (the 101st would have, in effect, four three-battalion infantry regiments when fighting in the ETO), the airborne divisions were significantly weaker than conventional divisions, particularly in heavy weapons.

This was not always appreciated by senior commanders, who tended to overestimate the length of line they could be expected to hold, and their ability to sustain themselves in prolonged combat. The determination of airborne units to make up in aggressiveness and stamina what they lacked in resources led to great heroism and high casualties.

D-Day

The 101st Airborne Division arrived in Britain in September 1943. By the eve of the Normandy landings Brig.Gen.Maxwell D.Taylor's "Screaming Eagles" had been augmented to include the 501st, 502nd and 506th PIR and the 327th and part of the 401st GIR, supported by the gunners of

the 377th PFA and 321st and 907th GFA Battalions.

The Division's first combat jump was made by 6,000 paratroopers, starting just after midnight on the night of 5/6 June 1944. The DZs were north of the town of Carentan, inland from Utah Beach; the 101st's vital mission was to hold corridors through the swampy ground behind Utah for the footsloggers of the 4th Infantry Division, assaulting from landing craft at daylight, and to advance south to Carentan to link eventually with troops moving inland from Omaha Beach.

Heavy enemy flak forced many of the C-47s carrying the Division to veer off course, scattering their sticks of paratroopers widely - some perished through drifting out to sea, others from being dropped dangerously low. Only about 2,500 men successfully assembled; units, parts of units and individuals were dispersed in the dark, with or without their equipment, over miles of strange countryside. It was a paratrooper's nightmare. Nevertheless, by early on D-Day the 101st had seized two vital exits from Utah Beach, linking up with the 4th Division at around noon.

Clearing German paratroopers of the 6th Fallschirmjager Regiment out of Carentan took five days of fierce fighting, however, followed by counterattacks by the 17th SS Panzer Grenadier Division. At around 4pm on 14 June the 101st linked up with 82nd paratroopers, finally joining the Omaha and Utah beachheads. There was to be no immediate rest for the 101st, however; they were sent into a new sector near Cherbourg before finally being relieved and shipped back to England on 13 July, after 33 days of combat.

Holland

After a few days' leave the 101st began a seemingly endless cycle of training and preparation for further operations, which were always cancelled - sometimes at the last moment - as the situation on the ground altered; no less than 16 operations were planned and aborted during August and September 1944. The next time the "Screaming Eagles" jumped it would be as part of the largest airborne assault in history: Operation "Market Garden", the joint US/British attempt to capture a long, narrow corridor leading over several strategic bridges in Holland, forming a path for the tanks of British XXX Corps into the German industrial heartland of the Ruhr. The southernmost sector, involving the capture of nine separate bridges and the holding of a 15-mile stretch of the strategic highway between Eindhoven and Veghel, was assigned to the 101st; northeast of them the 82nd would jump near

Nijmegen, and at the far tip of the operation British 1st Airborne would jump at Arnhem.

The simultaneous airlift of three divisions strained the Allied transport fleet beyond its limits - the operation would involve a total of 4,700 aircraft, and the 101st alone needed 424 C-47s and 70 gliders. Because of this, and an optimistic estimate of the time it would take the British tanks to fight their way up the single available road, only infantry would land in the first wave: the 502nd and 506th near Zon, half way between Eindhoven and Veghel, and the 501st around Veghel. The first wave of the Division, some 6,670 strong, began dropping at around 1pm on 17 September 1944 in the face of vicious flak. In the northern sector the bridges around Veghel were quickly taken; but the vital bridge over the Wilhemina Canal at Zon was blown by the Germans when men of the 506th were only 50 yards from it, and another important bridge at Best was blown next day despite desperate fighting by the 502nd.

On the 18th hundreds of gliders braved rain, mist and flak to land heavy equipment and 2,656 more troopers. A parasupply drop was less successful, leaving the 101st with the seeds of a serious ammunition, fuel and ration problem. After frantic efforts by British engineers the Zon bridge was replaced that night, and British armor began passing over early on 19 September. The 502nd and 327th took Best; but bad weather and German flak and fighters disrupted that day's landings by more troops and artillery. Heavy Waffen-SS counterattacks hit several points along the narrow and terribly vulnerable Allied corridor, as US paratroopers and British tankers fought together to preserve the fragile link. Often it was cut, to be retaken at grim cost. It was to be 23 September before the last elements of the 101st landed; and the 26th before the road in the 101st's sector was finally secured. By then the strategic plan was history; on the 25th the survivors of British 1st Airborne began to withdraw from Arnhem, after taking 80 per cent casualties.

Still there was to be no rest for the 101st; on 2 October they were sent north past Nijmegen to fight between the Waal and Lower Rhine rivers. It was not until 27 November, after suffering 2,118 casualties during 73 days of combat, that the Division was pulled out of the line and sent to a French rest area.

Bastogne

On 16 December 1944 Hitler's armies launched their last major counteroffensive in the West, driving through the weakly

held sector in the forested hills of the Ardennes. The terrain limited the Panzers to only a few possible roads, and capturing road and rail junctions was of central importance. One of the most strategically placed was the little town of Bastogne, which Eisenhower determined must be held at all costs. It was garrisoned with elements of the 9th and 10th Armored Divisions; and although the 101st had not yet regained its strength after the losses in Holland it too was ordered to Bastogne, commanded in Gen.Taylor's absence by Brig.Gen.Anthony McAuliffe. By early on 19 December sizeable elements of the Division were in place around Bastogne, after a tiring forced march through scenes of confusion.

Determined German attacks from several directions by the elite Panzer Lehr Division, 2nd Panzer and 26th Volksgrenadier Divisions soon involved the infantry of the 501st, 502nd, 506th, and 327th and the gunners of the 321st Artillery, supported by tankers and tank destroyers, in heavy and sometimes costly fighting. Positions in outlying villages were driven in. By the 21st the Division was reported to be completely surrounded and cut off; and that night the snow began to fall. Rushed to Bastogne, the 101st troopers were short of many necessities, particularly support weapons, and faced unknown numbers of enemy tanks from two good divisions. The next day a German party approached a 327th GIR position under flag of truce with a demand that the defenders of Bastogne surrender. McAuliffe's succinct response - "Nuts!" - passed into Airborne legend.

The 23rd brought a successful parachute supply drop, but also further damaging attacks; more positions were lost, and the perimeter shrank once again. On Christmas Day a major attack from the north-west saw gunners, cooks, drivers and clerks fighting as infantry; with help from tank destroyers and artillery it was driven off. Further attacks on the 26th were repulsed, despite Luftwaffe air strikes - a rarity at this date; and that afternoon the first relieving Shermans of the 4th Armored Division fought their way in from the south to make contact with engineers of the 326th Battalion. The ferocity of the fighting did not slacken, however, and see-saw battles raged throughout early January after the Division went onto the offensive. It was 18 January before Corps headquarters returned to Bastogne, presenting the 101st with a wryly worded receipt for the town in "used but serviceable" condition. Withdrawn to a quieter sector on 14 February, the 101st were honoured on 1 March with the first 9

Reconstruction: paratrooper of the 1st Brigade, 101st Airborne Division in II CTZ, Vietnam, 1965. His Ml steel helmet has the Ml-C parachutist's liner with distinctive web A-straps. He wears OG-107 fatigues displaying full-color shoulder sleeve insignia, insignia of rank, name and US Army tabs. His fatigue trousers have been modified by the addition of patch cargo pockets. M1956 LCE is worn in typical fighting order with various attached items: plastic one-quart canteen, M26Al fragmentation grenades, angle-head flashlight, 0-ring snap link for rappelling from helicopters, wet weather poncho liner rolled in an early rubberized poncho, etc. He has a slung "Claymore" bag for extra ammunition and personal gear, and carries the early M16 rifle with three-prong flash suppressor. (Photo courtesy Tony Mottram, from "Vietnam: US Uniforms in Colour Photographs" by Kevin Lyles, ISBN 1872004520, pub. Windrow & Greene Ltd., 1992)

Presidential Unit Citation ever awarded to an entire division.

In April 1945 the Division moved up to and across the Rhine, and during the final weeks of the war in Europe made a breakneck advance deep into Germany. On 5 May they reached Hitler's summer lair at Berchtesgaden. In August the 101st pulled back to France; a planned return to the USA was forestalled by the Japanese surrender; and on 30 November 1945 the Division was inactivated.

Reconstruction of a UH-1 helicopter door gunner, 101st Aviation Battalion, Vietnam, 1969. The shoulder insignia is still proudly worn in full colors, although a subdued version was now available. Over the third-pattern tropical fatigue uniform he wears door gunner's and crew chief's front-and-rear "chicken-plate" armor - officially, the 1968 Body Armor, Fragmentation, Small Arms Protective, Aircrewman, with nylon-covered ceramic plates in external pockets. He wears the 1965 AFH-1 Crash Ballistic Protective Flying Helmet, and 1968 fire-retardant flyer's gloves. (Photo courtesy Tony Mottram, from "Vietnam:US Uniforms in Colour Photographs" by Kevin Lyles, ISBN 1872004520, pub. Windrow & Greene Ltd., 1992)

Post-War Reorganizations

The next eleven years saw the 101st activated and inactivated three times as a training center division. Finally, in September 1956 it transferred to Ft.Campbell and rejoined the ranks of the active army. The reborn 101st Airborne Division was the first formation to test the US Army's new concept of the "pentomic" division. Broadly, this rested on the theory that no conventional division could fight as a single entity on the nuclear battlefield of the future; and that divisions should therefore have five separate combat groups each formed by an enhanced infantry battalion, capable of independent operations. In the 101st the core units of the five combat groups were the 2-187th, 1-327th, 1-501st, 1-502nd, and 1-506th; the artillery was similarly organized in five separate batteries. (This marked a break in the proud traditional lineage of combat regiments.)

The pentomic concept proved in practice to raise many difficulties, chiefly of manpower and firepower, service support, command and control; and as early as 1959 the Army began planning yet another reorganization. Meanwhile in 1958 the XVIII Airborne Corps was designated as the Strategic Army Corps - the spearhead for rapid deployment - with the 101st Airborne and 4th Infantry Divisions as its first-line elements. In 1961 the new divisional concept, termed ROAD ("Reorganization Objective Army Division"), was announced, and the 101st was converted in 1964.

The ROAD airborne division was a flexible structure capable of supporting a mix of manoeuvre battalions, the exact order of battle depending upon the assigned units and the task. Basic components in the 1960s were three brigades each of three infantry battalions, each of HHC and three rifle companies (four, in Vietnam); divisional artillery with three battalions, each of HHB and three howitzer batteries; a light tank battalion, armored cavalry squadron, aviation, engineer and signal battalions; and a divisional support command grouping various maintenance, supply and medical elements. The key was flexibility, and there could be rapid cross-assignment of units between brigades and divisional troops as demanded by the tactical situation. Although it varied due to different attachments, basic strength was around 15,000 men.

Meanwhile, during 1963, a highly significant program was being carried out at Ft.Benning by the so-called 11th Air Assault Division (Test). Their brief was to test the concept, techniques and equipment for an airmobile division capable of transporting a third of its combat units in a single helicopter lift. The program was extremely successful, and provided cadres for the new 1st Cavalry Division (Airmobile), which was formed in 1965 largely from the redesignated 2nd Infantry Division.

Vietnam

The 1st Brigade of the 101st Airborne Division, fully jump-qualified, landed at Cam Ranh Bay, Republic of Vietnam on 29 July 1965. The Eagle Brigade was initially assigned the role of "fire brigade" in II Corps Tactical Zone, usually being headquartered at Phan Rang in southern II CTZ; but in the two-and-a-half years that the brigade fought as a separate organisation they became known as the "Nomads of Vietnam", deploying in three of the four CTZs, travelling some 2,500 miles, and engaging in 26 different operations. Component units were the 1-327th, 2-327th and 2-502nd Infantry, and 2-320th Artillery.

First blooded in August 1965 in Operation "Highland" along Highway 19 between Qui Nhon and An Khe, the brigade had a harder and costlier fight in "Gibraltar" the following month, meeting NVA troops for the first time. Operation succeeded operation: "Van Buren" in Phu Yen Province, alongside Korean Marines; "Hawthorne" around Kontum; with Task Force "Oregon" in Quang Ngai and Quang Tin Provinces; "Klamath Falls" back in the southern II CTZ. A valuable innovation was the formation by each battalion of "Recondo" reconnaissance platoons, skilled in patrol and ambush work.

The remainder of the 101st Division began arriving in Vietnam in November 1967. In the meantime it had been hard-pressed in its task of providing airborne-qualified replacements for its 1st Brigade and the 173rd Airborne Brigade in Vietnam; the Army had an acute shortage of parachute-qualified personnel due to the constant drain of casualties, the short one-year tour of duty, and the competing demands of the 82nd Airborne and Special Forces. The 2nd Brigade (1-501st, 2-501st, 1-502nd) went to Cu Chi; the 3rd (3-187th, 1-506th, 2-506th) to Phoc Vinh; and the Division HQ to Bien Hoa. The 3-506th was attached to the 1st Brigade between late 1967 and July 1968.

The Division was, from the first, widely dispersed in I and III CTZs as "fire brigades" which were rushed from one trouble spot to the next. During the enemy's Tet Offensive of early 1968 the 101st had elements fighting from Quang Tri to Saigon, over 400 miles away; one platoon found itself fighting Viet Cong **11** commandos at the US Embassy in downtown Saigon.

Although the Division was seldom to serve as one formation, many elements were airlifted into the A Shau Valley for Operation "Somerset Plain" in August 1968. They were back there between February and May 1969, seeing heavy fighting in Operations "Massachusetts Striker" and "Apache Snow". During May three 101st battalions took terrible losses during the notorious battles for Ap Bia Mountain - "Hamburger Hill".

In mid-1969 the long-discussed difficulties of simultaneously satisfying the demand for jump-qualified troopers for the 82nd, 101st, and other airborne organizations led to the decision to convert the 101st into an airmobile formation like the 1st Cavalry Division. There was very little practical call for classic parachute assaults in Vietnam; only one such operation was in fact carried out throughout the war (Operation "Junction City", by 845 troopers of the 173rd Abn.Bde., near Katum on 22 February 1967). After a brief existence as the 101st Air Cavalry Division the converted formation was redesignated 101st Airborne Division (Airmobile) in August 1969.

The airmobile concept gave the Division a greatly increased helicopter force for inserting, extracting, and supplying troops in the field. Small forces of one or two companies would be inserted into suspected enemy territory; if contact followed other units would be airlifted into blocking positions; helicopter gunships took the place of artillery, and were in fact called "aerial artillery" units. For larger operations troops and airlifted artillery could be placed to block routes or valleys in the path of large-scale sweeps. Many such operations were conducted - some with conspicuous success - before the Division began withdrawing from Vietnam between December 1971 and February 1972, redeploying home to Ft.Campbell. The 101st was the last US Army division to leave the combat zone of Vietnam; elements of the "Screaming Eagles" had been in-country for nearly seven years.

*   *   *

On returning to Ft.Campbell the Division's 3rd Brigade went back onto jump status, carrying on the traditions of the inactivated 173rd Brigade; but this only lasted until 1974, and on 4 October that year the formation was definitively redesignated 101st Airborne Division (Air Assault). The "Airborne" title was retained for purely traditional reasons; only Pathfinder and other small necessary elements have since been maintained on jump status.

The 101st became part of the Rapid Deployment Force (formed in 1978; later, US Central Command) in 1980. It has since conducted many readiness and deployment exercises in the USA, Europe, and elsewhere, in environments as different as the Arctic and the Egyptian desert. In 1983 the Division was reorganized under a new regimental system; henceforth the three infantry brigades took on the identity of the 327th, 502nd and 187th Regiments. The first and second were two of the original units assigned to the Division in 1942; and the 187th holds the distinction of being the only airborne unit to fight in World War II, Korea, and Vietnam.

Memorial to the 248 members of the Division's 3rd Battalion, 502nd Infantry who were killed in an aircraft crash at Gander, Newfoundland on 12 December 1985 while returning from peacekeeping duties under the UN in the Sinai Desert.

THE WAR IN THE GULF

On 10 August 1990, eight days after Iraq invaded Kuwait, Major General James H.B.Peay III received orders to deploy his 101st Airborne Division to Saudi Arabia. The first advance elements arrived the following day. In the expectation that the first troop units to arrive might be thrust into combat as soon as they arrived, an infantry/aviation task force was organized for the first airlift, with the rest of the Division to follow. The airlift began on 17 August, with initial units deploying in defense of the airfields at Dahran and Damman.

This task force included the Division's ready battalion, two battalions of AH-64 Apache attack helicopters, a battalion of 105mm field artillery, part of the air cavalry squadron, a company of CH-47 heavy lift helicopters, and an assortment of other helicopters for command and control and electronic countermeasures. The only other US forces in place were one brigade of the 82nd Airborne Division supported by a battalion of Apaches. The members of the task force had no illusions about their ability to withstand an all-out Iraqi invasion: their best hope would be to blunt and delay it.

By early September the 2nd ("Strike") Brigade had been airlifted to Saudi Arabia; the 3rd ("Rakkasan") Brigade were flown in by the 17th. The 1st ("Always First") Brigade were the last to deploy. The rest of the Division's

helicopters and ground vehicles arrived by sea in late September.

Once in place, the first mission for the 101st was to act as a covering force in the path of any Iraqi invasion of western Saudi Arabia. A base camp was set up at King Fahd Airport, about 200 miles south of the Kuwait border near the coast, and two Forward Operating Bases (FOBs) were established closer to the border. In addition to the 101st's own units an additional aviation brigade, an armored cavalry brigade, and two field artillery brigades were attached to the Division. Intelligence indicated that facing the 101st on the other side of the frontier were one Iraqi mechanized and two infantry divisions. The Division's task was to slow down any Iraqi invasion as much as possible, and then to "hand off" the battle to its sister XVIII Corps formation to the south, the 24th Infantry Division (Mechanized); the 101st would then protect the 24th's western flank.

Conditions in the FOBs were very primitive, and the strain of possibly imminent combat was constant. The Division established a rotation schedule for the brigades to keep them fresh; each brigade spent 30 days in the FOB areas and 15 days back at base camp. The months spent at the FOBs were used for unit as well as combined arms training, including a rigorous program of night

One of the divisional MP battalion's Humm Vee vehicles, with M60 machine gun mounted, patrols the desert near the 101st's base camp in Saudi Arabia. Infiltration attacks against unit base areas were always a possibility, and the threat was taken seriously. (Photo courtesy 101st AA Division)

and live-firing exercises. By mid-November the flavor of the training exercises had changed, from defensive to offensive operations.

As the UN deadline of 15 January 1991 approached with no sign of Saddam Hussein ordering his invaders to withdraw from occupied Kuwait, there was a renewed fear that he would try to catch the Coalition off guard by launching an invasion. The heavy armor of VII Corps was not yet completely in place. A brigade task force from the 101st was formed to reinforce the 1st Cavalry Division. Heading out from their base camp, the 2nd Brigade moved 3,800 men, 700 vehicles and 80 aircraft more than 300 miles across the desert in less than 48 hours. The Iraqi attack never came; and on 17 January 1991 the Coalition air assault began.

A little-known fact is that helicopters from the 101st fired the first shots of the air war. Eight AH-64 Apaches from the

13

The months spent in Saudi Arabia during the Coalition's "Desert Shield" build-up saw intensive training for desert warfare. The first invasion plan had the 101st air-assaulting into a town, so urban combat was heavily stressed in early exercises. The plan was later changed to a landing in uninhabited desert, to reduce the high risk of casualties in house-to-house fighting. These troopers wear Desert Battle Dress Uniform (DBDUs) and helmet covers with regular green ALICE equipment and, in one case, temperate woodland-pattern PASGT body armor covers.
(Photos courtesy 101st AA Division)

Ten days before the ground war began the 101st began to fly reconnaissance missions into Iraq, scouting out the best location for FOB Cobra and the route the ground reinforcements would have to follow to reach it. A week before the Coalition advance the helicopters began attacking bunker complexes found along the route. They were also used to capture prisoners for interrogation about other Iraqi positions in the area - and not just in ones and twos, either. One large complex which would have prevented the ground convoy from reaching Cobra was located, and when it was destroyed the 1st Battalion, 327th Infantry captured over 400 prisoners. These revealed the location of other troops, bunkers and air defense sites that could have caused heavy casualties if they had remained undiscovered.

On the night of 23 February 1991, the day before the Allied ground advance, long-range surveillance teams were inserted by helicopter into the area selected for FOB Cobra to monitor Iraqi

1st Battalion, 101st Aviation Brigade, escorted by four US Air Force MH-53J special operations helicopters, knocked out two early warning radar sites deep inside Iraq, to clear a path of electronic darkness and silence into enemy territory for Allied strike aircraft. The mission was a complete success; none of the helicopters even came under fire while over Iraq.

As soon as the air war began the Division moved to a position 500 miles north-west of their base camp and just six miles south of the Iraqi border - this would be the jump-off point for their invasion of Iraq. The operation was scheduled to begin on 24 February with the establishment of a large Forward Operating Base, codenamed "Cobra", some 50 miles inside Iraq, with the ultimate objective of cutting the main road between Baghdad and Kuwait.

military activity. Others were placed along the flight path with electronic beacons to guide the Division's helicopters over the flat, featureless desert.

The invasion was originally planned for the early morning darkness, but the winter weather had other ideas. Because of fog the first task force, made up of elements of the 1st Brigade, did not lift off until almost 0730, in full daylight. While the landing at Cobra itself was unopposed, AH-1 gunships and US Air Force A-10 Thunderbolt II ground attack aircraft engaged an Iraqi battalion dug in less than two miles north of the LZ. Once they were on the ground A Company, 1-327th Infantry, along with C Battery, 2-320th Field Artillery, also pounded the complex; and more than 300 Iraqis surrendered.

With FOB Cobra secure its mission as a refuelling point could begin. This was vital if the following brigades were to reach their objectives in the Euphrates River valley and cut Highway 8, the only major artery between Baghdad and Kuwait. By the night of the 24th the Division's 1st and 2nd Brigades were solidly established at Cobra.

The 3rd Brigade planned an air assault on the night of 24/25 February to block Highway 8 just south of the Iraqi town of Al Khidr; but again, due to bad weather, the mission was delayed until full daylight on the 25th. The brigade was reinforced by a task force made up of two artillery batteries, three anti-tank companies, and two mounted rifle companies. Their mission was to stop any reinforcements heading south from Baghdad, and to prevent any Iraqi troops retreating from Kuwait. The infantry - 1,000 troopers in 66 UH-60A Black

Hawks - began their assault at 1500 hours. Landing safely, they set about cratering the road, blowing bridges and setting up ambushes.

The continuing bad weather left the infantrymen of the 187th on their own throughout the night of 25/26 February. The supporting force of artillery and anti-tank units had been lifted in to a position from where they could assemble and drive to the objective. Unfortunately the winter rains had turned the desert into a quagmire, delaying their progress. Sitting in the cold, wet desert darkness without their supporting units, the infantry spent a tense and uncomfortable night waiting for Iraqi troops to attack from either or both directions - a classic Airborne dilemma. Fortunately only a

few vehicles approached the road blocks, and these were dealt with in short order. The next day the supporting task force arrived with the heavy weapons. On the night of the 26th the rest of the brigade landed. A few skirmishes followed, but no major attack materialized.

For the 101st the final action of the war took place on 27 February, when elements of the 1st and 2nd Brigades established an FOB a hundred miles due east of Cobra; this new base, FOB Viper, would allow the Division to engage any Iraqi forces which managed to retreat from the holocaust which had now engulfed them in Kuwait. The war ended the next day, however, with the Division seeing no further combat.

(Right) The OH-58C Kiowa was used by the air cavalry squadron and attack helicopter battalions in the Gulf. Given the almost featureless flatness of the desert the Kiowa was not needed in its normal role of scouting for the AH-64 Apaches: the latters' advanced electro-optical systems allowed them to "see" better than the Kiowas. The OH-58Cs carried out air-to-air protection duties instead, being fitted with Stinger anti-aircraft missiles to counter any Iraqi helicopter threat and flying flank guard for the Apache formations.

(Below) AH-1 Cobra gunship flying low over the desert. The Cobras of the 2-17th Air Cavalry spent many hours inside Iraq before the invasion, scouting locations and ground reinforcement routes for the planned FOB. They were also instrumental in suppressing Iraqi ground fire, and capturing prisoners for intelligence-gathering.

(Above) An AH-64 Apache flies low over the dunes; while the desert terrain enabled the Apaches to use all surveillance and target-acquisition systems at maximum range, it also rendered them highly visible during daylight hours. (Photo courtesy McDonnell Douglas)

(Left) A crew from 1-320th Field Artillery loading a 105mm howitzer in a Saudi desert position. The Division's artillery helped establish FOB Cobra deep inside Iraq, hammering a nearby enemy battalion bunker complex into surrender. (Photo courtesy 101st AA Division)

(Right) CH-47D Chinook from the 101st's medium helicopter battalion landing at FOB Cobra during "Desert Storm". The sand took a heavy toll of the helicopters; engine life was reduced and many parts - rotor blades, brakes, windshields, tyres, etc. - had to be replaced much more frequently than during temperate area operations. A special engine air filter was designed, built, and delivered before the ground war began. (Photo courtesy 101st AA Division)

(Above) The tracks of the Apache...the remains of an Iraqi T-62 tank. The AH-64 attack units of the 101st were inside Iraq up to ten days before the Coalition ground invasion, attacking bunkers, air defense sites, trucks, and any armor which might interfere with the Division's operational mission. (Photo courtesy 101st AA Division)

(Above & below) War booty captured in the Gulf and brought home to the museum at Ft.Campbell. The AFV is a Brazilian-made Engesa EE-ll ten-man armored personnel carrier; the artillery piece is a Soviet-made D30 122mm howitzer - one of the literally thousands of Iraqi guns, some of them with superior capability to most Coalition artillery, which gave the planning staffs serious headaches during "Desert Shield". In the event, US airpower wrote this asset down to such a degree that it hardly hampered the ground advance.

(Above) Part of the display of captured Iraqi uniforms and gear at Ft.Campbell's Don F.Pratt Museum.

AIR ASSAULT SCHOOL

(Above) Students try rappelling down the 34-foot wall for the first time, under the watchful eyes of instructors. After a few attempts they will begin to enjoy it, realizing that their chances of getting hurt are small.

(Right) The "Australian rappel" is not a tactical technique, but is taught in order to build confidence; it is the biggest psychological hurdle for a student on the wall to overcome. If he makes a mistake he usually slams head-first into the wall, and finishes up hanging upside down.

(Left) The 25 instructors at the Air Assault School are among the Division's most highly qualified personnel.
(Photo: Fred Pushies)

(Right) The soldiers at the base of the wall hold the rappel ropes securely; letting go is one of the great sins of this stage of the course - tension on the rope stops the rappeller's progress if he happens to fall.

21

The heart of the 101st is the Air Assault School. As many as 90,000 US and foreign soldiers of all ranks and specialties have passed through the school since its inception in January 1974, learning the new techniques and building up the confidence required for this unique type of operation. The course is just eleven days long - but men who should know say that it is tougher than paratrooper jump school.

Each class begins with 170 students, divided into platoons and companies; officer students are put in command positions within the class. The curriculum is organized into three sections: combat assault, rigging and sling loads, and rappelling.

The first section teaches helicopter-related combat assault techniques and mission planning. Students learn the capabilities of the various types of helicopter, and how to work with and around them safely and efficiently. Apart from the classic air assault students are also instructed in pathfinder operations, setting up landing zones, and aeromedical evacuation. Practical sessions take place both in daylight and by night. Mock-ups of helicopter cabins are used to teach loading and unloading techniques. The final exercise is a night combat assault, planned and executed by students, using UH-60A Black Hawks.

During the rigging and sling load section the students learn how to prepare and rig equipment to be suspended under various types of helicopters. This is

(Top) During the demanding preparation and rigging phase of the course, two students and an instructor attach the rigging for a jeep to a hovering Chinook's middle cargo hook. If they forget to touch the hook first with a grounding device they will get a considerable electric shock from the static build-up caused by the rotor blades. It takes some practice to get used to working immediately underneath a huge, deafening helicopter that bobs up and down constantly, in rotor-wash that has earned the CH-47 the nickname "Big Windy".

(Left) Rappelling is taught as a means of tactical insertion in terrain which is too broken or wooded to allow helicopters to land. Obviously, it is not used in the presence of enemy forces, since the hovering helicopter presents a stationary target for ground fire.

(Left & Below) Male and female troopers sample the joys of the Ft. Campbell assault course. Female soldiers serve in many divisional units which see active service in combat zones during operations, e.g. the MPs. (Photos: Fred Pushies)

considered the toughest section of the course, due to the amount of information which has to be memorized. Students have to master the proper preparation and rigging of every item of equipment that the Division slings under a helicopter; to understand the tensile strengths of ropes, chains and straps; how to load each type of helicopter, and how to rig hook-ups to them. One night and two daytime exercises are conducted with CH-47 Chinooks, with every student performing each function of a rigging team. The final test involves each student examining a piece of equipment that is already rigged but with an unknown number of mistakes. The student has to identify at least three out of every four mistakes, correct them, and then have the re-rigged load lifted successfully. Mistakes in this section are not tolerated: a rigging error can cause a helicopter to crash.

The last section of the course covers rappelling out of a helicopter. The students begin on a twelve-foot inclined wall, before moving on to a vertical 34-foot wall and tower. Safety procedures are rigorously enforced, and students who fail to follow them quickly find themselves on the receiving end of intense, not to say deafening one-to-one attention from an instructor.

The importance of the strict safety rules becomes obvious when the students move on to the next phase: rappelling out of a UH-60A hovering 90 feet above the ground. A carelessly handled rope can fly into the rotor blades with disastrous results. A soldier who has not mastered the proper technique for attaching himself to the rope could plunge 90 feet to the unforgiving ground. The first rappel is performed without combat gear, the second with full pack and rifle. This training segment is also useful for the helicopter crews, to attain and hone proficiency in air assault techniques.

The final test is a twelve-mile march, in full field combat gear, which must be completed in three hours or less.

While the students come from units throughout the US Army, the instructors must be members of the 101st. Competition for the 25 positions is intense; after a rigorous examination an additional four months' training is required for soldiers who are accepted as new instructors. They must become rappel masters, qualify as pathfinders,

and earn their jump wings. The prospective instructor must then pass through the Air Assault School once again as a student; the instructors give him "special attention" to test his abilities and resolve, before he can proceed to specialised instructional training. When his tour as an instructor is finished he is one of the most highly trained members of the Division, and is considered a major asset by his next unit.

For two hours at a time a pair of Black Hawks pick up students, hover at 90 feet while they rappel down the ropes, then land for the next sticks. A rappel master stays in the helicopter at all times, to make sure the students are hooked up correctly and follow proper technique. Instructors on the ground on each side of the Black Hawk guide the rope-handlers and load the students; inattention could cause a rope to end up in the rotor blades, with potentially disastrous consequences.

INFANTRY, ARTILLERY, AIR DEFENSE

A field artillery captain discussing target location with a forward observer. Batteries may be placed remote from the main body of the infantry units they support; an infantry company is usually detailed as a cover force. Note that in these exercise photographs the personnel all wear the Multiple Integrated Laser Engagement System. The MILES rig comprises a harness with round black detectors and battery packs mounted over the helmet and torso, and a transmitter component - which can be coded to the range and power of various weapons - mounted at the muzzle. The detectors accurately register "hits" during a simulated firefight by triggering a light and a buzzer, and turning off the victim's laser transmitter until it is switched on again by an umpire. This allows more objective assessment of the results of an engagement than the traditional violent argument.

The M47 Dragon is the rifle platoon's medium anti-armor weapon; two launchers are carried by the platoon headquarters, the missiles being issued in their disposable launch tubes as rounds of ammunition. The launcher has day and night sights, the AN/TAS-5 night tracker detecting the target's thermal signature. Although no longer able to guarantee a kill against the frontal quadrant of the latest main battle tanks, the shaped-charge Dragon still gives the platoon unprecedented anti-armor firepower and high hit probability at maximum ranges of between 1,000 and 1,500 meters.

(Photo: Fred Pushies)

As with many aspects of the 101st, the organization of the infantry units within the Division is unusual. The three brigades each have three battalions, of the 327th, 502nd and 187th Infantry respectively. In each battalion the HHC and three rifle companies are conventional; each of the latter comprises a headquarters element, a mortar section with two 60mm M224s, and three rifle platoons each with two M60 machine guns, two M47 Dragon anti-tank launchers, and three rifle squads each made up of two four-man fire teams and an NCO leader. But in the 101st the battalions each have a fourth company: a TOW anti-tank company with 20 Humm Vees divided between five platoons. This gives each brigade 60 TOW vehicles.

Being the only motorized ground combat units in the Division the TOW Humm Vees are given a wide range of assignments. While their primary mission is anti-armor they are often tasked to perform reconnaissance, route security, and convoy escort duties. The vehicles' main armament can be switched from TOWs to M60 machine guns or Mk 19 40mm grenade launchers - much more suitable for close-in fighting against infantry or softskin vehicles - depending on the given mission.

The 101st's field artillery is all towed; self-propelled guns would be too heavy

Disadvantages of the Dragon are the sitting position, which makes concealment more difficult during the period when the tracker has to follow the wire-guided missile's flight to the target, and the visibility of the flaming back-blast.
(Photos: courtesy Fred Pushies & 101st AA Division)

for helicopter airlift. The Division's artillery brigade has three 105mm howitzer battalions of the 320th FA each with three batteries of six tubes; there is also one battery of eight 155mm howitzers from the 5-8th FA for long range and high value targets. The Division uses its artillery in two ways: the raid, and the deliberate attack. For the raid a helicopter drops a gun, crew and ammunition at a spot from which they rapidly get into action and open fire on a specific target. They are then extracted by helicopter as soon as the last round is fired, and shifted to another point before the enemy can react. In the deliberate attack the Humm Vee towing vehicle is also slung, attached to the howitzer, under a CH-47 carrying the crew; the crew and weapon are thus able to manoeuvre on their own as soon as they are landed.

The 320th FA are currently replacing the reliable old M102 105mm howitzer with the new M119 of the same caliber, a British-designed weapon which has about 3,000 meters greater range than the M102 (14,300m as opposed to 11,000m) for only an extra 200 pounds weight penalty. The 320th received the first American-made models of the new howitzer, which will eventually replace all the 105mm towed weapons in the 82nd Airborne and the Light Divisions of the US Army.

The air defenses of the Division, provided by the 2-44th ADA Battalion, are also undergoing modernization. One battery from this battalion is assigned to each of the three brigades. Each battery has a mixed inventory of 20 Stinger shoulder-launched heat-seeking missile teams, and nine towed M167 Vulcan six-barrelled 20mm "Gatling"-type rotary cannon. The headquarters battery fields an additional 20 Stinger teams which can be assigned to divisional units according to need. The Vulcan, whose 3,000rpm rate of fire and 1,600 meter effective range make it a versatile ground weapon apart from its ADA role, is nevertheless being phased out, to be replaced by the Avenger system. This is a pair of quadruple Stinger launchers mounted on a Humm Vee, giving a greatly increased air defense capability over the 20mm cannon: it can fire on the move, has longer range, and is more effective at night. The battalion began taking delivery of the Avenger in March 1993, and will eventually have 46 Avengers and 40 Stinger teams.

Air defense has a very high priority in the 101st; because of the Division's mission aircraft will often be the first enemy assets encountered, and the 101st's helicopters represent a very high value target for any enemy. Stinger teams are always included in the first lift into a landing zone.

(Opposite) A rifleman and a SAW gunner in tall grass reminiscent of Vietnam, in one of the manoeuvre areas around Ft.Campbell; such close cover enforces extra vigilance during tactical exercises, which the soldiers of the 101st take very seriously. Each of the two four-man fire teams in the infantry rifle squad includes a sergeant team leader with an M16, a grenadier with an M16 mounted with a 40mm M203 grenade launcher, a SAW (squad automatic weapon) gunner, and a rifleman who also carries at least one LAW anti-armor weapon. The M249 SAW, a development of the Belgian FN Minimi, takes the same 5.56mm rounds as the M16 rifle but has a greater effective range (1,300 meters); it takes either a 200-round belt in an assault magazine, as here, or the same 20- and 30-round box magazines as the squad's rifles, giving useful commonality of ammo supply in combat.

(Top) Millersville training area is named after the Division's current commanding general, Major General John Miller. This complex is used for urban warfare training, which is increasingly being emphasized in the US Army today. More and more, units are training for low- and medium-intensity conflicts, as opposed to the high-intensity, armor-heavy operations in central Europe which were the primary scenario during several decades of the Cold War.

(Left) The fire team grenadier's weapon, the M16 fitted with the M203 grenade launcher - here, with the MILES device mounted at the muzzle of the rifle. The 40mm grenades, with an accurate range of up to 350 meters, are aimed using the standard rifle foresight and an extra folding sight mounted on top of the barrel. The pump-action launcher adds about three pounds to the weight of the rifle, apart from the weight of the grenades, usually carried in a special 24-round vest.

(Below) A soldier applying the camouflage cream that is mandatory for all ranks and duties when units are "tactical".

(Left) Typical of the formidable long-service professionals who ramrod the combat units of the 101st is Sergeant Major Donald Purdy of the 3rd Battalion, 187th Infantry, photographed here in Millersville wearing regular US Army woodland-camouflage BDUs and ALICE load-carrying gear. His subdued insignia include rank on cap and collars; the Ranger qualification tab above the 101st shoulder sleeve insignia; and on the left chest the Combat Infantryman's Badge, Master jump wings, and the Pathfinder badge.

(Above) The 101st train extensively for night operations, which multiply the uncertainty and disorientation inevitable in any combat situation. After the first burst of fire from your weapon your hearing is impaired and your night vision is gone; it takes a high level of discipline not to fire at anything that moves - and thus give your position away to the enemy. (Photo courtesy 101st AA Division)

(Left) An Engineer officer keeping track of developments in the 101st's Assault Command Post during Exercise 'Mega Gold'. (Photo: Fred Pushies)

(Right) Close-up view of the M220A1 TOW launcher; the top sight is a thermal imaging device for night combat. As the missile leaves the tube two ultra-fine wires connecting missile and launcher are reeled off spools. All the gunner has to do is keep his target centred in the crosshairs, and signals are passed down the wires to guide it to the target; it is essentially jam-proof. However, with a maximum range of 3,750 meters the gunner and launcher are necessarily exposed for up to 20 seconds - a long time to sit and wait for return fire.

A TOW gunner atop his vehicle; note also the SAW - each platoon is issued two for local defense. The TOW Humm Vee has a three-man crew: driver/ammunition bearer, squad leader, and gunner. The vehicle normally carries one missile in the tube and six reloads in the back; during "Desert Storm" crews crammed in and strapped on extra rounds. The system can fire any of the different models of TOW now in the US Army's inventory.

(Above) The M996 TOW Missile Carrier. The TOW Humm Vees of the infantry battalions' fourth companies can be prepared quickly for air transportation; with the tube in place, it can be in the air in 10-15 minutes. Once back on the ground it can be moving off the LZ in under one minute - all that has to be done is to lay the rigging out of the way. The CH-47 can lift two vehicles and crews at once; the UH-60 can lift one, though that takes it close to its maximum gross weight. The launcher can be dismounted and used with a ground tripod that is carried in the vehicle, freeing up the Humm Vee to mount a machine gun or grenade launcher for the more mobile duties to which - as the 101st Division's only ground combat vehicles - they are often assigned.

(Left & below) An M60 machine gun being test-fired on one of Ft.Campbell's 39 firing ranges. This 7.62mm veteran of Vietnam is still widely used, although replaced as the squad weapon by the SAW; two guns are carried by the rifle platoon headquarters element - it has an effective range of 900 meters when using the bipod, and 1,800 meters when mounted on a tripod for sustained fire tasks. The M60 can be mounted on a wide variety of vehicles, and is the standard door gun for the assault transport helicopters. Door gunners must first qualify during daylight, then practice night firing without night vision goggles, and finally with these aids. They begin on regular ground ranges, progressing to firing from a UH-60 on the ground, and then pass an air-to-ground firing course.

(Top) Part of a 105mm artillery battery in the field; while the plastic camouflage netting stretched over the bulldozed gunpits and the vehicles does not blend perfectly with the dried grass, it does mask what is underneath from aerial reconnaissance - hopefully, for long enough for the intruder to be shot down or driven off. Concealing an artillery battery is a difficult proposition; each battery has six howitzers, 13 Humm Vees and four 5-ton trucks, and a large open area is needed in order to be able to direct fire in any direction.

(Bottom) Each howitzer has a Humm Vee prime mover, which can carry 30 rounds of ammunition along with all the other equipment needed by the crew to live in the field and fight their weapon for several days. This often leads to overloading, but the Humm Vee has earned the praise of the toughest critics - the soldiers who have to use it - for its ability to stand up to this kind of abuse.

(Top) Dug into the sands of Saudi Arabia, one of the Division ADA's M167 Vulcan 20mm anti-aircraft cannons. A derivative of the gun found in almost every US fighter aircraft built since the 1960s, it can fire at rates of either 1,000 or 3,000 rounds per minute, in bursts of 10, 30, 60, or 100 rounds; there is no mistaking the sound of this weapon if you are anywhere near when it fires. It has a limited effective range of only 1,600 meters, however, and lacks night and bad weather capability; it is currently being replaced by the Avenger system of quad-Stinger launchers mounted on a Humm Vee. (Photo courtesy 101st AA Division)

(Bottom) Five-ton ammo truck of the 320th FA; too heavy to be lifted by helicopter, the trucks follow in a ground convoy once the FOB and a traffic route have been secured. Above the cab is mounted the venerable, but still irreplaceable M2 .50 calibre heavy machine gun, its world-famous outline disguised here by a blank-firing device and a night sight. (Photo: Fred Pushies)

The other component of the 101st's mixed ADA batteries is the Stinger shoulder-fired AAMS, issued as a round of ammunition in a disposable launch tube requiring no maintenance or testing. An "all-aspect" missile, it does not have to be fired directly at the hot engine exhaust in order to lock on to the aircraft's heat signature - it can be launched from any angle including head-on, and still track and destroy the target. With a range of 5km and a flight speed of Mach 2, it is a reliably deadly defense for the infantryman - as it has proved in combat, in Nicaragua and particularly in Afghanistan. In the 101st the Stinger teams - some of whom go in with the first wave of the air assault to provide immediate protection on the LZ - consist of a team chief and a gunner; they have a Humm Vee to carry six reloads and all their personal gear and weapons. Proper placement of the teams is essential: they need a good field of fire while remaining concealed - they are a high priority target, for obvious reasons.
(Photo courtesy 101st AA Division)

AVIATION BRIGADE

What sets the 101st apart from any other division in the world is its aviation brigade. Because of the importance of helicopters to its mission the Division often receives the first models of new types. The brigade consists of eight battalions, plus an air cavalry squadron - a total integral fleet of 348 helicopters.

There are three battalions of AH-64 Apache attack helicopters - the premier attack helicopter in the world today. Its sophisticated vision and targeting systems allow it to detect and track targets from many miles' range, by day or night. Its weapons systems give it the ability to hit those targets from outside the accurate range of most light anti-aircraft weapons. The Apache is just as effective in low-intensity conflict situations, and is an excellent weapon against guerrilla or infiltration threats; the Division has run many exercises

during which Apaches detect and track, from long range, individuals moving at night.

During "Desert Storm" the 1st Battalion, 101st Aviation Regiment pioneered the use of extended range fuel tanks, with 230-gallon tanks mounted on the Apaches' weapon pylons. It was by using this system that the 1-101st attacked radar sites deep inside Iraq to open a corridor for Coalition strike aircraft on the first night of the air war. In just two days these Apaches travelled 1,500 nautical miles - a previously unheard-of achievement for a helicopter.

The 101st's three assault helicopter battalions fly the UH-60A Black Hawk, which was developed to replace the immortal UH-1 Huey. The Sikorsky designers took all the lessons learned from the Huey's service in Vietnam, and put them into the UH-60A. It is faster, more manoeuvrable, and capable of absorbing tremendous punishment - both

View from the cockpit of a UH-60A Black Hawk. Desert flying is a challenge, by day or night. While the helicopter is provided with sophisticated navigation equipment, the ground units requesting the helicopter usually are not, and may not know their exact location; the crew may have to search for them in flat terrain, exposing their ship to ground fire.

from enemy fire and from its pilots.

In addition to delivering troops to the battlefield (it accomodates up to eleven fully equipped infantry and a three-man crew), the Black Hawk can carry up to 8,000 pounds of equipment slung from a belly cargo hook. Artillery and vehicles are common loads, as are fuel bladders and ammunition.

The heavy lift role is performed in the 101st by a medium helicopter battalion

Even though the Apache has armor plate in many vital areas, the crews don't want to test it: this AH-64 is crossing a clearing discreetly below treetop level. Hugging the ground eventually becomes second nature to the pilots; in Iraq they flew at high speed as low as 15 or 20 feet above the sand.

Trio of Apaches lurking at a Forward Operating Base. Its avionics make the AH-64 the best choice for a high-intensity conflict such as defeating an all-out armored attack; but it is also ideal for low-intensity operations, and has proved its ability to track small groups of infiltrators at night.

(Top) Apache launching a Hellfire missile. In addition to tracking the target illuminated by the laser designator on its launch ship, the Hellfire can find targets illuminated by designators on the ground or aboard other helicopters. This versatility allows the launch helicopter to bob down behind cover after firing, exposing itself only for the minimum period.

(Photo courtesy McDonnell Douglas)

(Bottom) The muscle of the AH-64 attack helicopter. At right, two Rockwell AGM-114A Hellfire anti-tank missiles - long range, highly accurate and devastatingly destructive. These "fire and forget" laser-guided weapons can be used to engage several targets in rapid succession at (classified) ranges thought to extend to as much as five miles; up to 16 can be carried at once by each Apache. A more usual ordnance load mixes fewer Hellfires with pods of any of various types of rocket, some dispensing up to ten submunitions each. This pod is for the standard unguided 2.75in. (70mm) FFAR.

(Above & right) With its warty, prehistoric-looking nose containing the various sensor and sighting devices the Apache is far from pretty, but it is very effective. The small top ball is the pilot's forward looking infrared (FLIR) sensor. The image is transmitted to a helmet-mounted "monocle", moving as the pilot moves his head, which gives him a "window" through the darkness of night. Below it are the daylight TV sensor, and the laser rangefinder and target designator.

of CH-47D Chinooks. This Vietnam-era veteran has been continuously up-dated over the years; the D-model developed in the late 1970s can lift twice the load of the original A-model. At more than 26,000 pounds, its maximum payload is actually 3,000 pounds heavier than the helicopter's own empty weight. Unique triple cargo hooks on the belly can carry a Humm Vee and a 105mm howitzer together, at over 140mph; alternatively, individual cargoes can be slung on each hook for delivery to three separate locations.

While the UH-60A has effectively replaced the UH-1 in most roles, there is still one battalion of Hueys in the 101st. Aside from their official role as command and control vehicles these helicopters perform many other chores, and are used to transport cargo and personnel around the Division in non-combat situations. If necessary they could still fly into combat, and they retain their door gun mounts. There has been talk for years of eliminating the Huey from the US Army inventory; but nobody has found another helicopter which can do what the Huey does as well and as cheaply. With the decrease in military budgets the talk is now of up-grading Hueys with new engines and avionics. The pilots say that when the last Black Hawk is finally retired, its delivery crew will fly home in a Huey...

The ninth aviation battalion, which serves as part of the divisional support command rather than the aviation

(Right) Apache refuelling at a FARP. For deep penetration strikes the AH-64 can carry an external 230-gallon tank on a weapon pylon; another option is to send UH-60 and CH-47 helicopters to a safe point behind enemy lines loaded with fuel, ammunition and missiles, providing the attack ships with a quicker turnaround than if they had to return to base. Just visible under the nose is the muzzle of the Hughes 30mm chain gun mounted on its articulated arms. The gun is controlled by helmet-mounted sights, turning as the crewman turns his head; once the target is designated the computer aims and fires the weapon. The AH-64 carries 1,200 rounds for the 30mm cannon, which has a rate of fire of just over 600rpm.

(Below) Overhead view of the UH-60A Black Hawk, here equipped with the External Stores Support System and a pair of 230-gallon fuel tanks. The cylinder just behind the main rotor is the infrared countermeasures device, to confuse heat-seeking missiles; the box mounted slantways on the side of the boom is a flare dispenser, used to offer them alternative heat sources.

brigade, has no helicopters, but is one of the most important: the maintenance battalion. Their job is to keep the Division's helicopters combat-ready in any and all conditions. Part of the battalion will be found at the Division's combat base of operations, the Forward Operating Base. Here they are responsible for maintaining and repairing helicopters in the field, performing major jobs such as changing complete engines and transmissions. Helicopters with battle damage can be repaired sufficiently to allow them to be flown back to the Division's major maintenance base in the rear areas. The battalion even have their own test pilots to fly these ships home (how would *you* like to fly a shot-up helicopter 100 miles across hostile territory?) Those that are too badly damaged to be flown can be lifted back by Chinooks, or are destroyed in place.

(Top) In addition to its many other duties the UH-60A is used by attack helicopter battalions as a search-and-rescue ship during deep penetration raids; it hangs back several miles, either airborne or on the ground, ready to rescue shot-down crews under the covering fire of the attack helicopters.

(Above) Head-on view of a Black Hawk with the massive-looking ESSS fitted, carrying twin 230-gallon tanks. The UH-60A is often used by field commanders as an airborne command and control ship.

(Right) The two keys to the 101st's tactical mobility: UH-60A over Ft.Campbell with a slung Humm Vee.
(Photo courtesy Sikorsky Aircraft)

(Bottom) Infantry rappelling from the UH-60A Black Hawk. This twin-engined replacement for the UH-1 Huey can lift more, carry it further, and do it faster; that it quickly won respect and affection from its crews is quite a feat, considering the loyalty commanded by the Huey. Note the crew door forward of the main cabin door, over the undercarriage, allowing the crew unrestricted entry and exit even with a fully loaded cabin. The rappelling ropes are now anchored to a chain secured to the cabin ceiling, rather than to the floor, as formerly; this gives a much quicker and easier exit for the troopers.

(Below left) Dusk on the Black Hawk flight line at Ft.Campbell. The Division prefers to make combat air assaults at night, and spends as much as a third of all flight time in night training.
(Photo courtesy Sikorsky Aircraft)

(Below right) Pilot wearing night vision goggles. The NVGs intensify existing light up to 20,000 times, allowing pilots and crew to see without using artificial lights. The image is displayed through a binocular device attached to the helmet just in front of the eyes; it appears as a grainy green and white television image.

(Above) CH-47D from the 101st Aviation Brigade's medium helicopter battalion flying low over the desert, using the terrain to hide, as best it can, from enemy gunners. The engines exposed high on the tail make them excellent targets for heat-seekers.

(Left) UH-60A medevac helicopter from the 326th Medical Battalion demonstrating a running landing, as used in dusty terrain. The idea is not to hover - which would kick up a cloud of dust, robbing the pilot of his view of the ground - but to come in tail low until the tail wheel touches. The pilot then quickly sets the main gear on the ground as it is engulfed by the following cloud of dust.

(Right) A pair of Chinooks move in to take on sling loads of jeeps during a training mission. The CH-47 can lift every weapon system in the 101st inventory, and its crew; with its big rear loading ramp it can even take a 105mm howitzer internally.

(Left) Starboard view of CH-47D Chinook; note the "Home Sweet Home" nose art just forward of the door gunner manning an M60. The Division has only one battalion of these invaluable workhorses; they get a lot of use, and reliability is vital. During "Desert Shield" and "Desert Storm" a total of 163 were operational, flying almost 17,000 hours between them; they had a mission-capable rate of 85 per cent in combat.

(Left) The main mission for the AH-1E Cobras of the 2-17th Cavalry is to cover the squadron's OH-58 scouts. A typical weapon load for the AH-1E is four TOW missiles (though four can be carried under each stub wing, as here), 300 rounds for the 20mm cannon, and as many 2.75in. rockets as can be carried while still allowing the ship to hover. The gunship's job is not to seek and destroy enemy targets, but to protect the scout by suppressing ground fire.

(Below) The original version was blooded over Vietnam in 1967, but the elegant "Snake" still has a lot to offer in its ECAS model, with the three-barrel M197 Vulcan 20mm cannon mounted under the nose and an advanced composite main rotor.

(Right) Cobra firing a TOW simulator, the smoke being blown straight down by the rotor downwash. The simulator gives an accurate smoke signature, and can be seen by ground troops; on manoeuvres this keeps the Cobra crews honest about the details of their mock attacks.

(Top) This OH-58C of the 101st Division had to make an emergency landing during an exercise at the National Training Center; trying to mask itself from the eyes of OPFOR, it backed into a ravine and the tail rotor struck some rocks. Despite the visible precautions, the crew were unhurt.

(Right) The OH-58C Kiowas of the air cavalry squadron are used as scouts for the Apache attack units; they are smaller, harder to see, and therefore harder to hit than the AH-64s - and, to be brutally realistic, if they do stumble into a hornet's nest they are less expensive to replace. At "point", the scouts' only defenses are flying ability, experience, and a high ambient level of suspicion. The Kiowas can only perform by day; they have no night flying aids other than NVGs for the crews.

Four "Snakes" living in the desert of the National Training Center, Fort Irwin, in southern California. This site offers the most realistic training available to US ground forces; units rotate through for three-week periods to fight different types of battles against a Soviet-style armored brigade simulated by OPFOR units. The Division regularly trains to live and fight in hostile environments, including Alaska during winter exercises.

An AH-1E with its engine panels open for a morning preflight inspection; ease of access makes inspection and maintenance faster in remote locations, and the desert sand and dust mandate frequent checks and replacement of some items.

(Left) The 101st's few remaining Hueys are mostly flown in support roles and for ferrying command staff around the Division. Notice the "bathtub" infrared suppressor, deflecting the hot engine exhaust gases up into the rotor blades for cooling. Many UH-1s are slated for conversion into UH-1V medevac ships, with more powerful engines and transmissions. Several companies are privately funding research into the Huey's potential for upgrades, and it is safe to bet that the US Army will still be using this immortal helicopter into the 21st century.

(Below) Wherever the helicopters go, the maintenance units follow; the Division sends an element of the aviation maintenance battalion to every FOB, where the mechanics can repair combat damage and replace components up to and including complete engines. Here the crew of a maintenance vehicle check out a CH-47.

(Above) For quick access to the Black Hawk's engine, transmission and other systems the front housing slides forward and other panels hinge outward, exposing the complete powertrain.

(Right) A Kiowa and Apache team cross an open clearing together in the early morning light. In fact, normal procedure is for the OH-58 to cross first and then radio the Apache to follow after checking out the route of travel.

(Below) Major field repairs to a Black Hawk are carried out with the aid of a lightweight crane.

SUPPORT COMMAND

(Above) Three CH-47 Chinooks refuel at a FARP in the California desert. The engines and rotors are kept turning during this "hot refuelling" process; a special closed circuit refuelling system prevents fuel spillage.

(Left) The 101st, with its special need to be self-sufficient, is the only division to have its own air ambulance company, from the 326th Medical Battalion; usually these are corps assets, distributed to divisions on an as-needed basis. The UH-60 medevac ships help establish forward hospitals with sling loads, leaving the other Black Hawk units free to concentrate on combat support.

Because the 101st must be self-sufficient, the support elements are of even greater importance than in other divisions. The helicopters - the heart of the Division - would be useless without quick refuelling and rearming. The efficiency of the Forward Area Refuelling Point (FARP) determines how far and how fast the Division can move. In the Persian Gulf the commanders quickly realized that the outdated equipment with which they arrived in theater could not sustain the Division. Equipment and personnel were mixed and matched, and commercial equipment was purchased to make the FARPs more efficient.

Some problems were much harder to solve, such as providing a method of controlling blowing sand at remote operating bases. The sand reduced engine power and, through its frighteningly abrasive effect on vital components, increased the maintenance workload. Nothing short of paving over the sand seemed to work really efficiently!

The unique structure and operational mission of the 101st provide their own unique support problems. How do you supply units that move 100 miles a day over difficult terrain? In the Gulf War the major combat elements secured Forward Operating Bases, which were then supplied by air until reached by a huge ground convoy escorted by attack helicopters. Each situation is unique, and calls for skill and ingenuity on the part of the support troops. 51

(Top) The patient carousel of a medevac UH-60; it can carry up to six litters on trays that can be moved up and down, and there is also provision for oxygen tanks. For space reasons the unit is usually set up for only four patients.

(Right) An injured trooper is loaded aboard a medevac Black Hawk. These helicopters are equipped with an internal rescue hoist to retrieve patients from terrain where the UH-60 cannot land; the 250ft. cable can lift loads up to 600 pounds. The Division has a complete field hospital, a more extensive facility than is usual due to the need for self-sufficiency. Casualty transport on the ground is by M997 Humm Vee ambulances of the 326th Medical Battalion, which carry four litter or eight ambulatory patients in a heated or cooled environment, depending upon circumstances.

(Below) A Forward Area Refuelling Point (FARP). Each of the bladders in the pit holds 500 gallons of jet fuel; portable generators power the pumps which transfer fuel along several flexible hoses from the bladders out to multiple stations where several helicopters can refuel at once, cutting down the vulnerable time spent at the FARP. A CH-47 can lift in seven full bladders slung from its cargo hooks.

(Bottom) This compact engineering vehicle, with a front loader and a backhoe, can be airlifted under a Chinook. It can quickly prepare firing positions for artillery or TOW Humm Vees, or make earthworks for troops.

(Right) This bulldozer - used by engineers for building firing positions, clearing landing zones, and even constructing runways for USAF fixed wing transports - can also be airlifted into a combat area under a Chinook.

(Below) A pair of M978 fuel servicing trucks; the Division owns a large number of these, to provide fuel for the helicopters in their staging areas, thus relieving congestion at the FARPs during rush hour. A large convoy of M978s made a dash across the Iraqi desert as soon as FOB Cobra was established in February 1991.

AIR ASSAULT

(Above & left) Because of the isolated nature of the 101st's mission, and their lack of integral armor, the Division works closely with USAF tactical assets such as the A-10 Thunderbolt II ground attack aircraft. Apart from "prepping" the Division's objectives, A-10s act as enemy aircraft during training exercises to give the ADA practice in target acquisition. When the 101st struck into Iraq in February 1991 A-10s helped to secure FOB Cobra.

It started in the distance: a low rumble that quickly grew in intensity, until it could be felt as well as heard. As it got closer it seemed to be coming from every direction at once. Indistinct shapes could be seen darting in and out of the treetops. Suddenly, a pair of slim, deadly Apache attack helicopters racketed between the trees and swept over the open field, searching hungrily for any sign that the enemy were lying in wait.

With the landing zone confirmed clear, wave after wave of Black Hawk assault transports swept in to unload their troops in a bewildering aerial ballet, each helicopter surging up again out of the dust after spending no more than 30 seconds on the ground. Among them, big twin-rotor Chinooks set down their dangling artillery pieces and anti-tank vehicles as protective gunships orbited the area, ready to pounce on any resistance. But there was none; and the troopers quickly set to work to organize a base camp and to prepare to move on their objectives....

An air assault is an incredibly complex

(Above & opposite) The troopers' insurance policy against air assaulting into a "hot LZ": the AH-64 Apache flies shotgun for the assault transports, and prowls the area of the LZ in search of enemy resistance before, during, and after they land. Here Apaches fire 2.75in. rockets; the pods are wired up to release various different salvo patterns, to taste. With relevant rocket types the Apache's laser rangefinder can be linked to the rocket to trigger precise release of submunitions. These views show to advantage the Apache's widely-spaced engines and advanced exhaust plume suppressors, to help baffle enemy heat-seekers; its "survivability" is also increased by various jamming and decoy devices. (Photos courtesy McDonnell Douglas & 101st AA Division)

(Right) OH-58C Kiowa scout of the Division air cavalry squadron checking out the brush in the area of the LZ. This Kiowa is equipped to carry two Stinger AAMS as defense against enemy helicopters.

operation to organize and execute. With its organic helicopters the 101st Division can transport three full battalions of infantry, with their associated weapons, in a single lift. Timing is obviously critical in an operation this complex: a group of helicopters that arrive too early or too late by only one or two minutes can upset the entire operation - and the danger of catastrophic collision over the crowded LZ is potentially ever-present.

It all begins with good intelligence, most of which is obtained by the OH-58C scout ships of the divisional air cavalry squadron. Landing zones must be found which are close enough to the objective to surprise the enemy, yet not so close as to bring helicopters and troops under fire as they land. Routes of travel must be established, making the best use of terrain to avoid enemy detection and fire.

The first in are the attack helicopters. They will protect the assault transports en route to the objective; take out any resistance in the area of the LZ; and then cover the transports as they land and depart. Once the troops are in place, they will provide fire support and intelligence during the ground assault.

Mixed in with the troop transports will be the heavy lift helicopters with their slung artillery pieces and vehicles, so that the infantry is left without heavy weapons support for only the minimum period after landing. The Chinooks are also essential for carrying cargo and fuel to the FOB that must be established to support the helicopter force near the troops operating on the ground. This allows them to refuel and rearm quickly before returning to support the ground assault.

(Above & right) The moment of truth: is the LZ hot? Is it a trap? The waves of Black Hawks touch, for no more than half a minute, and even with 60 pounds on their backs the troopers race for cover as if their lives depend on speed - which they just might.
(Photos courtesy Fred Pushies & Sikorsky Aircraft)

This might be described as an "Iraqi's eye view" of the Apache, and helps explain the previously unheard-of phenomenon of large numbers of enemy infantry actually surrendering to hovering helicopters. The Apache's structure and systems are armored to survive hits from 12.7mm and 23mm weapons, and the long-stroke landing gear and the cockpit seats are designed to absorb the shock of crash landings.

Once the initial air assault is completed, the helicopter force must be prepared to move troops and equipment at short notice as the ground situation develops. Troops can be moved to cut off retreating enemy elements, block the approach of reinforcements, or extract friendly troops in danger of being overrun. Artillery units are constantly being moved from point to point, to maintain their support for the infantry while avoiding the threat of enemy counterbattery fire. The central idea of air assault is that no matter which way

the enemy turns, he will face a powerful force on the ground. Properly executed, the mission of the 101st can lead an enemy commander into thinking that he is fighting several divisions at once.

In the 101st the air assault is never really considered completed until the Division has been relieved, and transported back behind friendly lines by its aviation brigade. Then the Screaming Eagles are ready to strike again - over great distances, in any direction, and against any enemy.

With the first wave of infantry, Black Hawks fly in immediate protection against enemy airstrikes: the new Avenger system, with two quad Stinger missile launchers mounted on a Humm Vee. (Photo courtesy Sikorsky Aircraft)

(Left) A company commander's headquarters can be as basic as a few square feet of flattened grass beside the LZ; here a captain checks in over the backpacked AN/PRC-74 radio. It is said that a company is the best command an officer can have throughout his career: small enough to know all his men, and to share their experience of combat, and large enough to challenge his command ability through some degree of tactical independence.

(Above) The M102 105mm howitzer, which saw extensive service in Vietnam from 1966, is in process of replacement by the M119 but is still in service. A pedestal between the wheels serves as the front support for firing, allowing rapid traverse. The two main ammunition types used in the 320th FA are high explosive and rocket-assisted, giving ranges of 11,500m and 15,000m respectively.

(Right) Chinooks lifting in M198 155mm howitzers. The Division's Battery C, 5-8th Field Artillery has eight M198s, used against high-value targets such as enemy armor units, ADA, and large logistic sites; they would not normally be employed against troops unless they were in large concentrations. The 155mm has a range of 18,150m with conventional ammunition, or up to 30,000m with rocket-assisted rounds.

(Above) CH-47D Chinook delivering a sling load of 105mm ammunition for the Division artillery. The D-model - which the 101st received before any other US units - is an almost completely factory re-engineered up-grade of the earlier A, B and C-models, with more powerful engines, improved transmission and rotors, modern avionics, and a modified cockpit taking account of modern night vision aids. It can carry up to 26,000 pounds - more than twice the load of the CH-47A. To see eight Chinooks shifting a whole artillery battery across country,

each carrying a crew and slinging a howitzer and a cargo net of ammunition, would make any old-time gunner officer weep with envy.

(Inset) For artillery raids a pair of UH-60A Black Hawks can lift two 105mm howitzers with their crews and ammunition - one slings the guns, the other carries the people. (Photo courtesy Sikorsky Aircraft)

(Above) While not as extensively used as resupply by landing at rapidly improved dirt airstrips, parachute delivery - as by this C-130 dropping a large palletized load - can be laid on. Not as much can be delivered by this method, but it does allow supply directly to a particular unit.

(Left) Part of an ADA TOW platoon deploy to cover the LZ. Each platoon has four TOW Humm Vees; a command and control Humm Vee used by the platoon leader and his radio operator; and a resupply Humm Vee, which the platoon sergeant rides with a driver and up to 20 extra rounds.

(Below) The operation is well under way, and the battle is being controlled from a well-camouflaged Tactical Operations Center. In the TOC it would not be unusual to find representatives from every other service: liaison officers from the USAF for close air support, from the USN for gunfire and aviation support, and from the USMC for artillery and aviation support and co-ordination.

(Top & above) Under the relaxed gaze of a 101st Division engineer dozer-driver, a rugged and reliable C-130 comes in and touches down on a dirt strip inside an established Forward Operating Base: by this stage of the developing operation the real estate that was once a potentially hazardous LZ has started to resemble "downtown".

The C-130 can deliver supplies, troops and equipment directly to the Division, off-loading fast and then flying casualties out for treatment in more sophisticated rear hospitals. The C-130s proved invaluable to the Division during the invasion of Iraq.

Printed in Singapore

This edition published
in Great Britain by
Windrow & Greene Ltd.
5 Gerrard Street
London W1V 7LJ

A CIP catalogue record for this book
is available from the British Library.

ISBN 1-872004-53-9